OREGON
impressions

photography by Charles Gurche

FARCOUNTRY PRESS

RIGHT: Broken Top Mountain in Three Sister Wilderness Area west of Bend.

TITLE PAGE: Wallowa Lake reflects the Wallowa Mountains in northeastern Oregon.

FRONT COVER: Multnomah Falls.

BACK COVER: The sandstone Pacific coastline at Cape Kiwanda.

ISBN: 1-56037-222-2
Photographs © Charles Gurche
© 2002 Farcountry Press

LEFT: Rock climbers tackle the heights at Smith Rock State Park near Redmond.

BELOW: In Oregon Dune National Recreation Area, north of Coos Bay on the Pacific.

FACING PAGE: A Seal Rock State Park sunset over the ocean.

RIGHT: Skiing from Mount Bachelor's summit.

FACING PAGE: Aspens take on a sunset glow in Winema National Forest.

LEFT: Haystack Rock in Cape Kiwanda.

FACING PAGE: Fiery morning awakening for the Deschutes River near Bend.

RIGHT: Reflections of Shaniko City Hall, which dates from 1901, in the window of the Shaniko Hotel.

BELOW: Canada geese on the Deschutes River.

FACING PAGE: Crater Lake in winter garb.

BELOW: An Oregon white oak tree in Wasco County.

FACING PAGE: Smith Rock State Park's granite cliffs rise above the Crooked River.

ABOVE: Portlandia, the hammered-copper figure on the Portland Building in that city, would be 50 feet tall if standing.

RIGHT: Vista House in Crown Point State Park offers views of the Columbia River Gorge.

BELOW: Steens Mountain aspens, aflame with autumn.

FACING PAGE: Near Lincoln City.

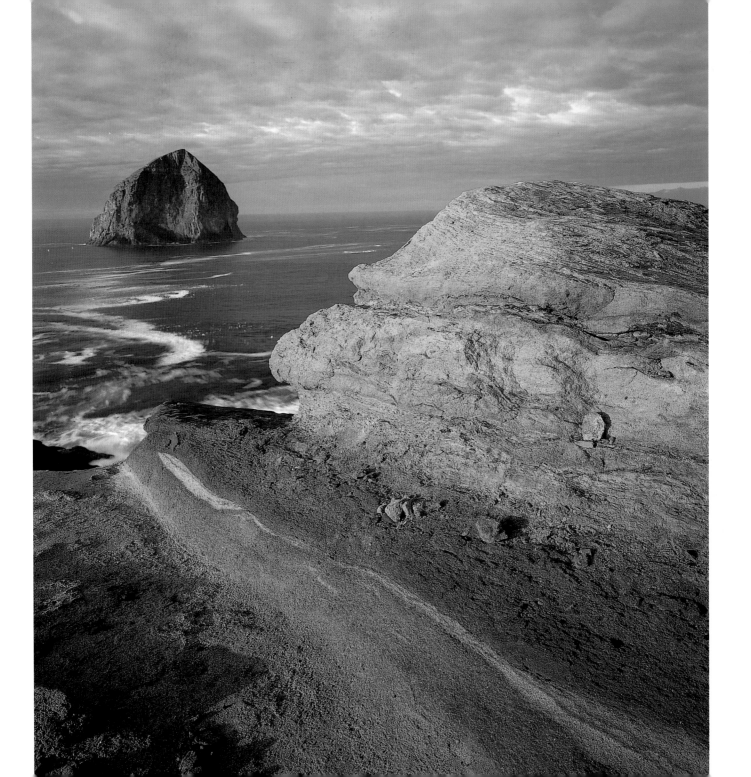

ABOVE: Classic colors on a Wasco County farm.

FACING PAGE: Yamhill County clover field.

BELOW: Moving sculpture in Oregon Dunes National Recreation Area.

FACING PAGE: Washington County wetlands waken to a foggy morning.

BELOW: Summit of southeastern Oregon's Steens Mountains.

FACING PAGE: Rocky coast near Pacific City.

Sparks Lake reflects "Charity," southern-most of the Three Sisters.

ABOVE: Klamath County aspens.

RIGHT: The Columbia River from Umatilla National Wildlife Refuge.

FAR RIGHT: Alpenglow on the South Sister.

LEFT: Portland and the Willamette River.

BELOW: Fairy Falls in Columbia River Gorge National Scenic Area.

RIGHT: Bigleaf maple leaves on a bed of ferns.

FACING PAGE: Rustic bridge at Wahkeena Falls, Columbia River Gorge National Scenic Area.

LEFT: The Pillars of Rome rock formations, Malheur County.

BELOW: Beach strawberry.

RIGHT: Astoria's Flavel House Museum is a restored 1885 Queen Anne mansion.

FACING PAGE: Old Town in Astoria.

ABOVE: Mount Jefferson rises above the Willamette National Forest.

FACING PAGE: Crater Lake's rocky rim.

Mount Hood's summit at sunset.

ABOVE: Spring flowers in the Columbia Gorge.

LEFT: A curtain of water veils a curtain of moss in the gorge.

RIGHT: Night begins to fall at Broken Top.

BELOW: A Bend cafe.

RIGHT: Mount Angel Abbey in Marion County.

BELOW: Permanent residents in Shaniko.

FACING PAGE: Reconstructed Fort Clatsop, near Astoria, shows how the Lewis and Clark Expedition wintered here, 1805-1806.

LEFT: **Lupine blossoms on Mount Hood.**

FACING PAGE: **Latourell Falls beautifies Guy W. Talbot State Park near the town of Bridal Veil.**

RIGHT: Owyhee River Valley badlands.

BELOW: Natural rock art on the Pacific near Tierra Del Mar.

The Three Sisters rise in Oregon's Cascade Mountains.

RIGHT: Beach boulder study near Woods.

BELOW: Harney County's historic Peter French Round Barn.

FACING PAGE: Owyhee River Canyon reflection.

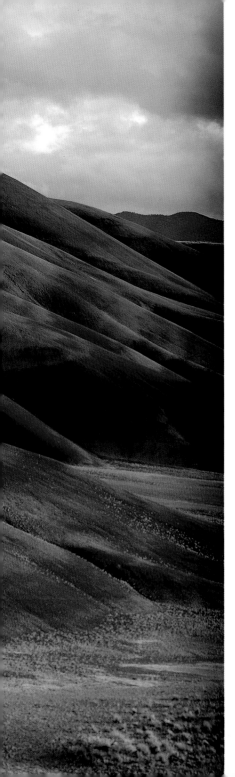

LEFT: The well named Painted Hills in John Day Fossil Beds National Monument.

BELOW: Petrified wood found near Burns.

55

Sunrise over the Columbia River Gorge.

RIGHT: Gordon Creek in Multnomah County.

BELOW: Tanner Creek Falls, Columbia River Gorge.

FACING PAGE: Punch Bowl Falls offers its libation in Columbia River Gorge National Scenic Area.

RIGHT: Gala apple harvest at Ontario.

BELOW: The Pine Tavern has served Bend diners since 1936.

FACING PAGE: Mount Hood takes on sunrise coloring.

BELOW: Competitors in the Oregon World Cup International Sled Dog Race near Bend.

FACING PAGE: Sitka spruce in a coat of fog, Siuslaw National Forest.

RIGHT: Red bell peppers are an Ontario-area crop.

BELOW: Red alder and vine maple near Sandy.

FACING PAGE: Alders along the McKenzie River leaf out for spring.

FACING PAGE : Buttercups fill a Hood River County field.

BELOW : Rabbitbrush above Crater Lake.

ABOVE: At the peaceful Elowah Falls in John B. Yeon State Park.

FACING PAGE: Washington Park's Japanese garden in Portland.

LEFT: Ecola State Park on the Pacific.

FACING PAGE: Quiet time in the marina below Astoria Bridge.

BELOW: Bee plants contour a hillside in John Day Fossil Beds National Monument.

FACING PAGE: Evening in Smith Rock State Park.

Heceta Lighthouse, north of
Florence, flashes Oregon's
most powerful ship's beacon.

BELOW: Marion County farmstead.

FACING PAGE: Stormy glory near Seaside.

LEFT: Springtime on land and sea, Florence.

FACING PAGE: Lake Billy Chinook in The Cove Palisades State Park near Madras.

Charles Gurche

Charles Gurche is one of the United States' foremost nature photographers. His work has appeared in numerous magazines, including *Audubon, National Geographic, Natural History,* and *Outside,* and in the books *Kansas Simply Beautiful, Missouri Simply Beautiful, Virginia Simply Beautiful, Virginia Impressions,* and *Washington Wild and Beautiful.*

As sole photographer, he has completed 70 calendars and six books, and has photographed for Kodak, the Sierra Club, Smithsonian Books, and the National Park Service. Awards have been presented to him by the Roger Tory Peterson Institute and the Society of professional journalists. For print information, email the photographer at: charlesgurche@msn.com

BELOW: Marion County farmstead.

FACING PAGE: **Stormy glory near Seaside.**